Meryl Doney

How the Bible came to us

Illustrations by Peter Dennis

A LION BOOK

Oxford . Batavia . Sydney

Copyright © 1985 Lion Publishing

Published by
Lion Publishing plc
Sandy Lane West, Littlemore, Oxford, England
ISBN 0 85648 574 8
Lion Publishing Corporation
1705 Hubbard Avenue, Batavia, Illinois 60510, USA
ISBN 0 85648 574 8
Albatross Books Pty Ltd
PO Box 320, Sutherland, NSW 2232, Australia
ISBN 0 86760 600 2

First edition 1985
Reprinted 1985, 1986, 1987, 1988, 1989

Acknowledgments
The following material appears by kind permission of the copyright
holders:
Cliff Richard extract (19) from *You, Me and Jesus*, published by
Hodder and Stoughton; Roger 'Bomba' extract (19) from Bible Pack
Factsheet P 11 © The Bible Society; other extracts on 19 by
permission of Campus Crusade for Christ International, Arrowood
Springs, San Vernadina, California 92414, USA.
John 3:16 in the different languages (16) is reproduced by
permission of The Bible Society, from their booklet, *The Story of
Bible Translation*.
The author would like to thank all those who have helped in the
preparation of this book, especially Hilary Morgan, Information
Officer of The Bible Society and Brian Fewings, Communication
Department, Wycliffe Bible Translators.

Illustrations of children on 1, 2, and 20 by D'reen Neeves.

Photographs from The British Museum (Rosetta Stone, 6, Codex
Sinaiticus, 7); The British Library (illuminated manuscript, 11, title
page, Coverdale Bible, 14); BBC Hulton Picture Library (Gutenberg
printshop, 12, coronation, 17); Sonia Halliday Photographs (Notre
Dame, rose window, 11); Israel Museum (Isaiah MS, 8); Lion
Publishing/David Alexander (Qumran caves, 8).

Library of Congress Cataloging in Publication Data

Doney, Meryl, 1985
  How our Bible came to us.
  "A Lion book." Includes index.
  1. Bible—Canon—Juvenile literature. 2. Bible—
Versions—Juvenile literature. 3. Bible—Publication and
distribution—Juvenile literature. (1. Bible) I. Dennis,
Peter, 1985 ill. II. Title.
BS465.D66 1985 220.4 84 28953
ISBN 0 85648 574 8

Printed and bound in Belgium

The Bible is probably the world's best-known book; it is certainly the world's longest-standing best-seller.

When the Good News Bible was published in 1976, the demand was such that it had to be printed a record twenty-one times in the first year. By 1979 it had reached the sixty million mark and taken the world record for paperback sales. Clearly the Bible still has something to say to today's world.

This book looks at the story behind the Bible and the reasons for its popularity. We also look at what is inside the covers and how to find your way around it.

The story of the Bible spans more than four thousand years of the world's history. All kinds of people, from different times, races and backgrounds have been involved. People have argued and fought over the Bible's message. It has changed whole nations and the lives of countless individuals. Men and women have been prepared to die in order to see it distributed as widely as possible. This story is one of the most remarkable and exciting in the world.

This is the world's number one best-seller.

FACTS AND FIGURES

The Bible appears three times in *The Guinness Book of Records*:
- It was the first-ever book to be printed mechanically.
- Called the Gutenberg Bible, one of the 21 surviving books from this printing also appears as the most expensive printed book ever to be sold. It raised £1,265,000 at auction in 1978.

- The Bible is also the world's most widely distributed book with some 2,500,000,000 copies between 1815 and 1975.

In one year the Bible Society report:
- sales of over ten million Bibles worldwide;
- four hundred million shorter portions of the Bible distributed.

Since the invention of printing, complete books of the Bible have been published in 1,763 different languages and dialects. But over two hundred million people in the world today still have no Bible in their language.

The Bible is the best-documented ancient text in the world. We have some 13,000 manuscript copies of portions of the New Testament.

CONTENTS

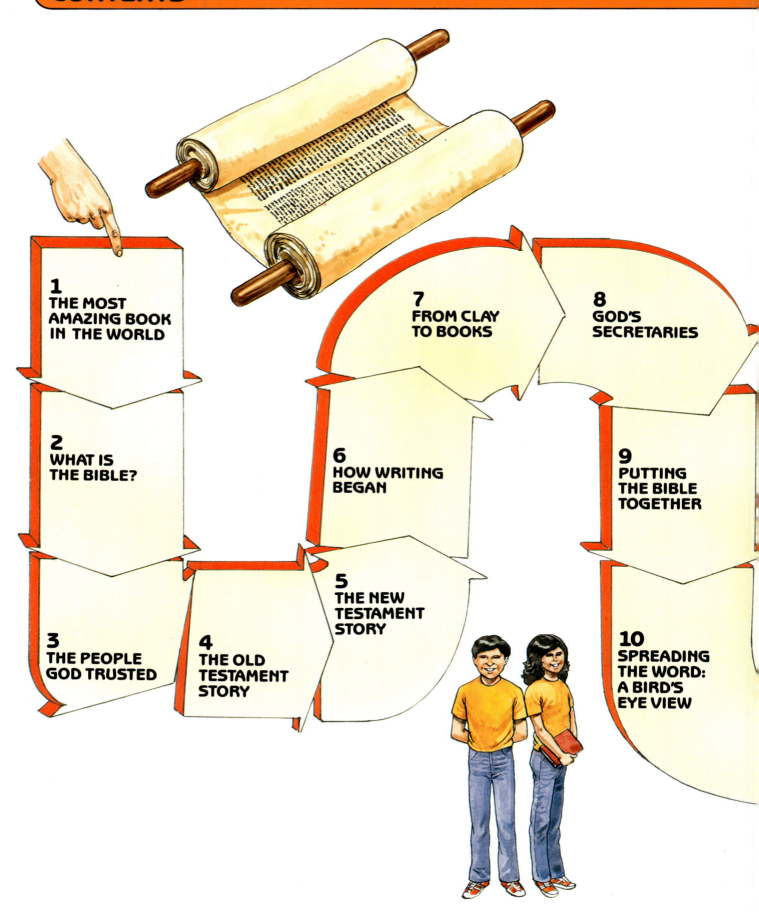

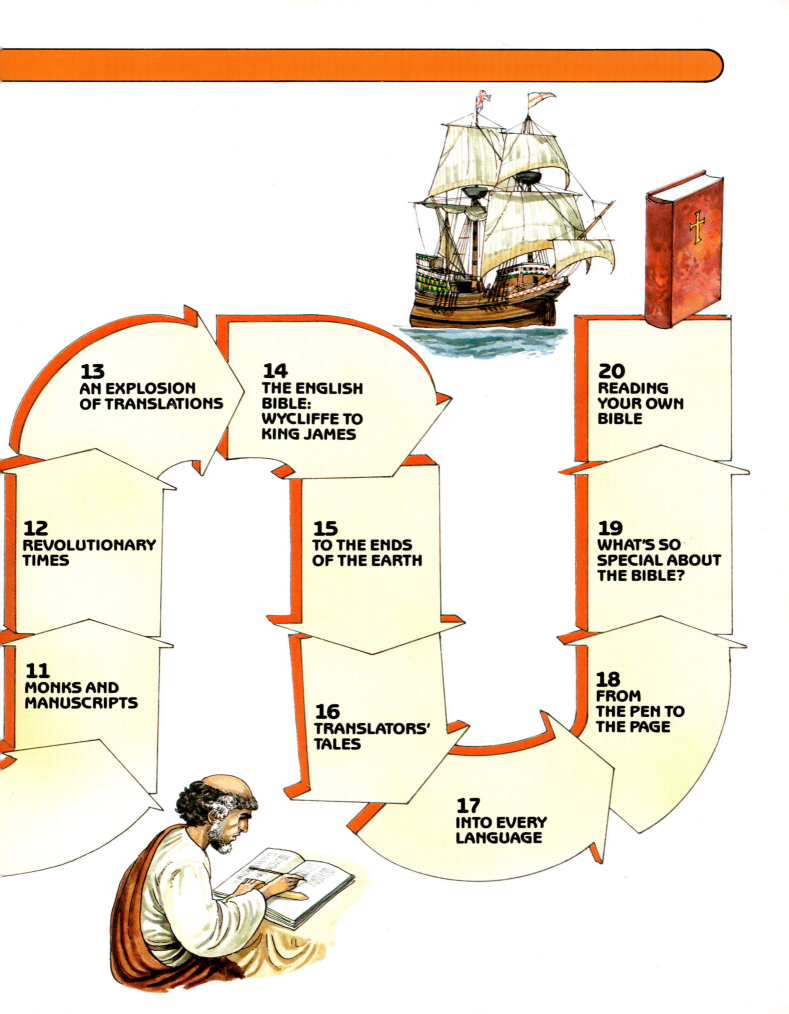

WHAT IS THE BIBLE?

Look, I've just borrowed this book.

That's not a book, it's a whole library!

The first surprising thing about the Bible is that it is not one book. It was not written by one person. It's a whole library of books!

The Bible we use today contains sixty-six books, written by very different people over a period of some 2,000 years. They include true stories and parables, songs and poetry, laws and rules, sermons and letters, events in history and predictions about the future.

In fact, there is so much in the Bible that you need some help to find your way around. Here is a picture of the Bible-library, with some notes on the books.

It is divided into two parts, the Old and New Testaments. The Old Testament is nearly twice as long as the New. It is about God's chosen people, the people of Israel, and takes us from the beginning of time, through the sad day, centuries later, when they were conquered and taken as prisoners to Babylon, to the time when the exiles returned home.

Then there is a break of several hundred years in the story. The New Testament begins with the birth of Jesus. It is about his life and the spread of the Christian church after his death and resurrection.

The Book of the Law

The first five books are called the Pentateuch, which means 'five scrolls'. It is really one book divided into five parts. It contains the history of God's people from Abraham to Joseph, with an introduction about the very earliest history of all — the creation of the world and the growth of civilization on earth. It also includes God's 'rules' called the Ten Commandments, and detailed instructions about daily living. The Jews call it 'The Book of the Law' or 'The Torah'.

Old Testament History

The next twelve books are history. They take the story on from Joshua and his famous battle of Jericho to the invasion and defeat of God's people by the Babylonians and Persians, and their return from exile.

Poetry and Wisdom

Next come five books of poetry and wisdom, which contain some of the best-known writings in the world. Job is a drama, the Psalms are poetry and songs for worship. Proverbs and Ecclesiastes contain wise sayings and the Song of Solomon (or Song of Songs) is a love poem.

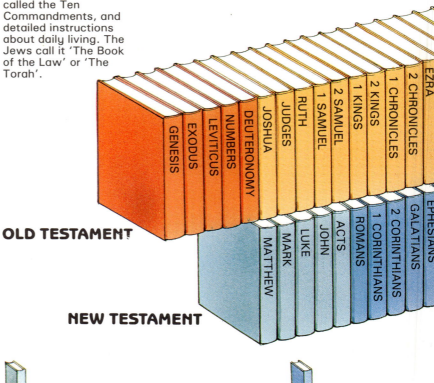

OLD TESTAMENT

GENESIS · EXODUS · LEVITICUS · NUMBERS · DEUTERONOMY · JOSHUA · JUDGES · RUTH · 1 SAMUEL · 2 SAMUEL · 1 KINGS · 2 KINGS · 1 CHRONICLES · 2 CHRONICLES · EZRA

NEW TESTAMENT

MATTHEW · MARK · LUKE · JOHN · ACTS · ROMANS · 1 CORINTHIANS · 2 CORINTHIANS · GALATIANS · EPHESIANS

New Testament History

The first four books of the New Testament are called 'gospels', which means 'good news'.

The aim of all four writers was to tell the story of Jesus before all those who had actually seen and known him died, so that people could have

an accurate record based on evidence from eye-witnesses.

Luke (the Greek doctor who went with Paul on his journeys) also wrote the story of how the church grew, called The Acts of the Apostles.

The Letters

A collection of twenty-one letters make up the rest of the New Testament. They were written by Christian leaders (thirteen of them by Paul) to the churches springing up all over the

The Prophets

The last seventeen Old Testament books are called the Prophets. They record the important messages preached by some of the special leaders God called to speak to his people. The prophets encouraged the people to worship God and warned of his punishment when they disobeyed and turned to idols. God enabled some of these men to look into the future and predict what would happen.

1 THESSALONIANS · 2 THESSALONIANS · 1 TIMOTHY · 2 TIMOTHY · TITUS · PHILEMON · HEBREWS · JAMES · 1 PETER · 2 PETER · 1 JOHN · 2 JOHN · 3 JOHN · JUDE · REVELATION

JOB · PSALMS · PROVERBS · ECCLESIASTES · SONG OF SONGS · ISAIAH · JEREMIAH · LAMENTATIONS · EZEKIEL · DANIEL · HOSEA · JOEL · AMOS · OBADIAH · JONAH · MICAH · NAHUM · HABAKKUK · ZEPHANIAH · HAGGAI · ZECHARIAH · MALACHI

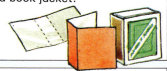

Revelation

Middle East. They contain teaching, encouragement and warm personal greetings, as well as some sharp criticism where the Christians were getting things wrong.

The last book is unique. Written in poetry and picture language, it is a series of visions of the future, designed to encourage and inspire the early Christians, against the background of Roman persecution.

GOD'S WORD

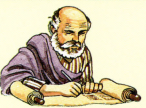

The Bible is different from any other book in the world for one very important reason. It is the work both of many different people and of God himself. The Bible says it is 'God-breathed'. We use the word inspired. This does not mean that God dictated his words to the writers, but that he inspired them or caused them to write the truth.

The Bible's words can therefore be trusted and its message has a special power to speak to people of every age and outlook. That is why the Bible is often called 'God's Word'.

MAKE YOUR OWN BIBLE LIBRARY

1 Collect 1 large kitchen matchbox and 6 small ones.

2 Cover each small box on 3 sides with coloured sticky paper, like a book jacket.

3 Cut 6 narrow strips of white paper and glue around 3 sides of each box. Draw lines for pages.

4 Write the different kinds of Bible books on the outsides: The Book of the Law, History, Poetry and Wisdom, The Prophets, Gospels and Acts, Letters and Revelation.

5 Cover the tray part of the large matchbox with brown sticky paper.

6 Label it 'Bible Library' and put in the books.

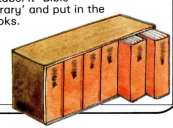

It would have been easy for God to choose one person and dictate to him or her all the facts about the world we live in and a long list of rules for the way we should live.

But this is not the way God works: he chooses to work through people. He chose individuals and groups, and worked in their lives so that they learned valuable truths about him through the things that happened to them.

The stories of their experiences and what they learned through them were then written down and handed on from one generation to another. As we read about them we can see God at work in real situations.

The very mixed bunch of people who feature in the Bible demonstrate clearly that God is interested in everyone, whatever we are like. Here are the stories of just some of the people God trusted with this message.

SOME OLD TESTAMENT WRITERS

Moses

God's people were slaves in Egypt when Moses was born. Baby Israelite boys were being killed, so his parents hid him in a basket at the river's edge.

He was rescued by an Egyptian princess and brought up at the palace. This was God's way of preparing a leader for his people.

When Moses grew up, God told him he had chosen him to lead the Israelites out of Egypt, back to Canaan, the land God had promised them.

It was to Moses that God gave the law — part of the first five books of the Bible.

David

David's story is a dramatic one. Brought up a shepherd boy, he was chosen by God to be king of Israel. David showed himself to be a brave soldier and a great king. He was also a gifted poet and musician, writing many of the most beautiful prayers and psalms in the Bible.

Isaiah, Jeremiah and Ezekiel

These were just three of the prophets — people to whom God gave a message at a time of special need. They called people back to faith when they took up pagan practices or when they were fearful of foreign invaders. The later prophets encouraged them in exile, and gave them a new hope for the future — a hope of a coming deliverer who would give them a new start.

Ezra and Nehemiah

Ezra was a priest and teacher of the Law at the time when most of God's people were captives in Babylonia under the rule of a Persian king. He was called by God to lead them back to their own country, to rebuild the temple and to persuade them to return to worshipping God.

Nehemiah had a top job at the king's court. He tells the story of God's calling to go back to Jerusalem and to repair the ruined city.

SOME NEW TESTAMENT WRITERS

Matthew

Matthew lived at the same time as Jesus. He was a tax collector, siding with the Romans and collecting money for them. The people hated him. Jesus saw him at work and called him to be a disciple. Matthew left everything to follow Jesus. Later, he wrote about Jesus in the 'Gospel of Matthew'.

Mark

John Mark was a young man when Jesus and the disciples met in Mark's mother's house in Jerusalem. He would watch them and listen to the teaching. He may have been present at the crucifixion. He certainly became a Christian and went with Peter and Paul on their missionary journeys. When he wrote his Gospel Mark probably drew on what Peter remembered.

Who wrote the Bible?

All sorts of different people.

Luke

Luke was a Greek-speaking doctor who journeyed with Paul. He carefully researched the life of Jesus and the story of the early church in his Gospel and the Acts of the Apostles, to explain the Christian faith to the non-Jewish world.

John

John and his brother James worked in their father's fishing business. They were probably disciples of John the Baptist before leaving him to follow Jesus. John was one of the small group of disciples who were closest to Jesus. Later he became a leader of the church. He wrote the Gospel of John, several letters, and may also have written the book of Revelation.

Peter

Peter and his brother Andrew, like James and John, were fishermen on Lake Galilee and joined Jesus early in his work. Peter soon became the leader of the twelve disciples, and later a leader of the church at Jerusalem. Two letters of Peter are included in the New Testament.

Paul

Paul was at first very much against Jesus. He was well educated, a top man in Jewish religious circles and a Roman citizen. He was on the way to arrest some Christians when he saw the risen Jesus. From that moment, he became a keen follower and missionary to the whole Roman world. His many letters form the largest part of the New Testament.

THE OLD TESTAMENT STORY

1250 BC

Moses is rescued by the princess of Egypt and brought up at the palace.

Moses leads the people's escape from Egypt, through the Sinai Desert to the borders of Canaan. God gives them the **Ten Commandments**.

Under their leader **Joshua**, the Israelites invade Canaan and gradually win possession of their 'promised land'.

The Israelites are **slaves in Egypt** for 400 years.

Ramesses II was probably the Egyptian king who had to let Moses and his people go.

Judges including Deborah, Gideon and the strong man Samson rule Israel, and free them from enemies.

The Old Testament begins: 'In the beginning when God created the universe . . .'

1750–1250 BC

Joseph is sold as a slave, but becomes Prime Minister of Egypt.

The Philistines The fierce 'Sea People' known as the Philistines held cities on the coastal plain. They were skilled workers in iron.

Adam and Eve lived in the Garden of Eden, in harmony with God. But they wanted to be free of him and go their own way. The 'fall' into sin was the result . . .

Noah and his family were saved from the great flood by building the ark.

Jacob (Israel) has twelve sons who become fathers of the twelve tribes of Israel.

The Egyptian civilization can be traced back as far as 3000 BC. From the paintings, inscriptions and models in their tombs, we have learnt a great deal about Egyptian culture.

1800 BC

By building the **Tower of Babel**, people tried to reach up to God. But the result was confusion and a 'babble' of different languages.

Abraham is called by God to leave his home city. God promises to make him the founder of a whole new nation.

The temple tower called a ziggurat was built by the king of Ur at about the time of Abraham.

2000 BC

1050 BC

The Israelites ask for a king: **Saul** is anointed by the prophet Samuel.

The boy given back to God by his mother Hannah grows up to become the prophet **Samuel**.

1000 BC

Shepherd-boy **David** becomes Israel's greatest king, after defeating the Philistine champion, Goliath.

950 BC

King **Solomon** realizes his father's dream to build a temple for God at Jerusalem.

900 BC

After Solomon's death, the kingdom is divided by **civil war**. The south, under Solomon's son, is called **Judah**; the north becomes **Israel**.

850 BC

Both kingdoms have a succession of good and bad kings. The people worship foreign gods.

750 BC

The Babylonians took control of the Assyrian Empire from 612 BC. King Nebuchadnezzar II captured Jerusalem in 586 BC and took the people into exile.

The Assyrians were fierce fighters, dominating many neighbouring kingdoms, including Israel and Judah. Scenes of victory are carved on their palace walls.

Tiglath-pileser III of **Assyria conquers Israel**.

550 BC

Daniel at the court in Babylon. **Ezekiel** encourages the exiles.

Jerusalem falls to Nebuchadnezzar II of Babylon. Judah is taken into exile.

The prophet **Jeremiah** calls the people of Judah to return to God.

God sends prophets to call his people back. But Samaria falls to the Assyrians: the **end of the Kingdom of Israel**.

600 BC

500 BC

Jews are allowed to **return home** and rebuild the temple.

The Babylonian Empire falls to King Cyrus of Persia.

Under Alexander the Great, **the Greeks** conquered the Persian Empire in 333 BC, built cities and theatres and spread Greek culture throughout the known world.

The vast **Persian Empire** extended from India in the east to Egypt and Greece in the west. When the Persian King Cyrus took over the Babylonian Empire in 539 BC he allowed the Jews to return to Jerusalem to rebuild the temple.

Under **Nehemiah**, the walls of Jerusalem rebuilt.

350 BC

Judea under foreign rule: Greeks 331–320, Egyptians 320–198, Syrians 198–63.

In 63 BC Pompey takes Jerusalem for Rome.

THE NEW TESTAMENT STORY

For 300 years the people of Israel had suffered under foreign rule — first the Greeks, who brought with them their own culture and civilization, then Egyptian and Syrian rulers, and last of all the Romans, who took control in 63 BC.

God's people longed for a saviour. Although there had been guerrillas and resistance movements, none had set them free. When would God keep his promise to deliver them, as the prophets had foretold?

The baby **Jesus** is born to Mary and Joseph in Bethlehem. God tells the shepherds and wise men that this is his promised Saviour-King.

0

King Herod dies: his three sons divide the country among them.

AD 20

John the Baptist announces the coming of the one God promised to send. John is beheaded by Herod Antipas.

Jesus begins to preach and teach. In three years that change the world he announces God's kingdom and demonstrates God's power in healing and forgiveness: people can be 'made new'.

AD 30

Jesus goes to Jerusalem to face death. He is tried on a charge of claiming to be God, and crucified. Three days later the grave is empty and he appears, alive, to many of his followers.

AD 60

Paul is imprisoned and taken to Rome. He writes many letters to the young churches.

Paul, the fierce persecutor, becomes a follower of Jesus, taking the good news of forgiveness and new life throughout the Roman world.

AD 70

Jerusalem is sacked by the Romans in AD 70. Many Jews are massacred and Christians flee.

AD 80

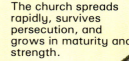

The early church is persecuted under the Emperor Domitian.

AD 100

The apostle John dies, around AD 100.

The church spreads rapidly, survives persecution, and grows in maturity and strength.

THE WORLD OF THE NEW TESTAMENT

The first-century world was ready for the good news about Jesus.

The Greek Empire, established by Alexander the Great, spread civilization throughout the known world. Greek became the common language, crossing national boundaries.

After years of war, the Romans took over the empire. Caesar Augustus brought peace and harsh, but fair, government to the whole region. The Romans were hard-working, well-organized people. They built a fine network of roads throughout their conquered territories. People — and ideas — could now travel freely and quickly.

And the time was ripe for new ideas. Greek and Roman religion had become empty and formal. The Jews were keenly awaiting the Messiah and liberation from the Romans.

Groups of Jews scattered throughout the empire served as natural starting-places for the first Christian preachers. They made good use of the fine new Roman roads and stable, peaceful conditions to spread the faith. And their writings — in everyday Greek — were soon being read in every corner of the world.

Beautiful Greek vases were often painted with scenes from everyday life.

Roman soldiers were stationed throughout the empire, to keep the peace.

The Romans built their roads to last, using layers of gravel and stones. Many still exist today.

The men who ruled in Rome in New Testament times:

 Caesar Augustus 27–4 AD was Emperor when Jesus was born

Tiberius AD 14–37 was Emperor when Jesus was crucified

 Caligula AD 37–41

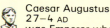 Claudius AD 41–54 was Emperor at the time of Paul's journeys

Nero AD 54–68 had many Christians killed

 Galba/Otho/Vitellius AD 68–69

 Vespasian AD 69–79

 Titus AD 79–81

 Domitian AD 81–96 persecuted the church

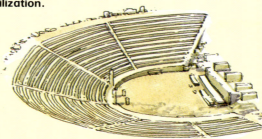

The Parthenon at Athens (reconstructed here) is a reminder of the greatness of Greek civilization.

The Greeks loved athletic competition. The Olympic Games began as a festival in honour of the god Zeus.

Most big cities in New Testament times had a theatre, one of the legacies of Greek culture.

HOW WRITING BEGAN

The need to transmit messages, keep lists, record promises and generally make our mark on things, is as old as civilization. So the story of the development of writing goes back to very early times, long before the invention of the alphabet.

1 Around 30,000 years ago, our prehistoric ancestors were painting scenes of men, animals and birds on the walls of caves. Examples of this first kind of 'writing' can be found all around the world, from Europe to Australia.

2 As civilization developed, rough drawings of objects began to be used in a more organized way, creating a simple picture writing.

3 5,000 years ago the ancient Egyptians evolved the beautiful, stylized pictures of the hieroglyphic script we can still see today on their tombs and monuments.

4 The Babylonians developed the pictures into simple shapes that could be pressed into soft clay, using a wedge-shaped stick. We call this cuneiform writing.

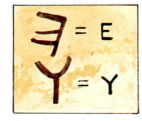

5 The next big step forward seems to have been made in Canaan, where an inventive scribe hit on the idea of an alphabet. He found that his language could be reduced to around twenty simple sounds. To each sound he gave a sign — usually chosen from a word beginning with that sound. Vowels were not written at first.

This first alphabet was so successful that it spread rapidly, and by 1000 BC many peoples had adapted it to their own language, including the Hebrews of the Old Testament.

Your writing's awful.

Well, it's still developing!

ALPHABETS GROW

We tend to take our alphabet for granted, as if it had always been that way. But letters have a long history. The ones we use today were developed thousands of years ago and in countries far away from our own. Take the letter A, for example.

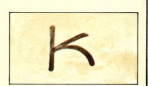

1 It began as the head of an ox.

2 In picture sign-writing it was simplified like this.

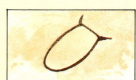

3 The earliest alphabet from Canaan used the ox-shape as the letter for the 'a' sound.

4 Written in the more rapid script of the Phoenicians it became this.

5 The Greeks slowly formalized it into their letter Alpha.

6 The Romans developed the letter we use today from the Greek.

THE ROSETTA STONE

In 1799 Napoleon led an expedition to Egypt. There, one of his men accidentally unearthed a large stone, covered in writing. It was probably the single most important discovery in the history of translation, because it held the key to crack the code of the Egyptian language.

The writing turned out to be a royal decree written three times — in two forms of Egyptian and also in Greek.

It took 23 years, but at last the experts were able to decipher the Egyptian and the whole world of that ancient civilization was opened up.

THE LANGUAGES OF THE BIBLE

Of course the Bible was not written in English! Because it was put together over thousands of years, by different people, it was originally written in several languages.

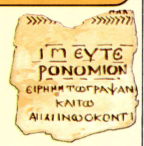

Hebrew
Most of the Old Testament is in Hebrew, the language of the descendants of Abraham.

The Hebrew alphabet has twenty-two letters but no vowels (these were later represented by a system of dots). It is read from right to left.

Aramaic
Parts of the book of Daniel were written in Aramaic. Closely related to Hebrew, it was the official language of the Persian Empire, and widely used for trade and diplomacy.

By New Testament times, Aramaic was the ordinary language of Palestine and Jesus would have spoken it. It is still used today by the villagers of Malloula in Syria.

Greek
The New Testament was written in 'common' Greek, the everyday language so widely used in the eastern part of the Roman Empire.

CRACK THE CODE

1 Late one night a metal object crashes to Earth. A message is written on it in two languages. One is a strange system of symbols. The other you recognize as English.

2 Use it to write the space alphabet in the boxes below.

A	B	C	D	E	F	G	H	I	J	K	L	M	N	O	P	Q	R	S	T	U	V	W	X	Y	Z

3 Now you can translate the message below.

_____

_____

_____

With the invention of writing came the possibility of keeping records and information for the future.

Many thousands of texts from Bible times and even earlier have survived until our own day. We have learnt most of what we know about the ancient world by deciphering them.

They were written on all kinds of materials. The Babylonians used small tablets of clay; the Egyptians used papyrus. Important inscriptions were cut into rock, or palace walls, or painted on the walls of tombs.

Eventually, cumbersome clay tablets and scrolls of papyrus gave way to more convenient forms. By the time the early Christians wanted to spread the new message, the ancestor of our 'book' was fully developed.

THE STORY OF THE BOOK

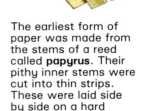

The earliest form of paper was made from the stems of a reed called **papyrus**. Their pithy inner stems were cut into thin strips. These were laid side by side on a hard surface, and another layer of strips was placed on top, at right-angles. The two layers were then stuck together by beating them with mallets.

Writing-boards were used by the Assyrians and were common in Greek and Roman times. The ancestor of the school slate, these boards were made of wood or ivory, with a wax surface for writing. Often two boards were hinged together.

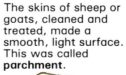

The skins of sheep or goats, cleaned and treated, made a smooth, light surface. This was called **parchment**.

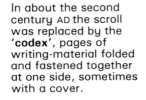

In about the second century AD the scroll was replaced by the **'codex'**, pages of writing-material folded and fastened together at one side, sometimes with a cover.

Christians may have been the pioneers of this early book, because it was easier to handle and transport.

It was soon discovered that papyrus sheets could be beaten together into long strips and rolled up for storage. These '**scrolls**' were the 'books' of Old Testament times. Scrolls were written from right to left (Hebrew or Aramaic) or left to right (Greek) in columns, and continued on the back if extra space was needed. People usually wrote with reed brushes, using black ink made from soot.

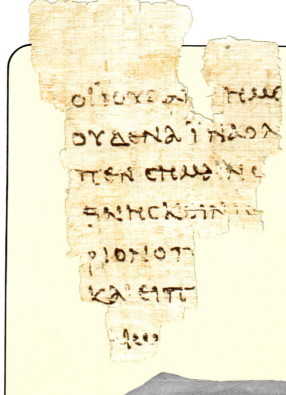

The earliest known fragment of the New Testament is a part of John's Gospel, written in Greek on papyrus. It dates from about AD 130.

Codex Sinaiticus, written in Greek on parchment, is the earliest complete manuscript of the New Testament. It dates from the fourth century AD.

Papyrus was expensive. For ordinary people, broken bits of **pottery** were the commonest writing-material. There were always plenty of pieces around and these 'sherds' were very useful for notes and lists, bills and receipts. They were the notelets of the ancient world!

MAKE YOUR OWN SECRET SCROLL

1 Cut a piece of plain paper into a long, thin strip.

2 With sticky tape, fix one end to a knitting-needle or a stick.

3 Roll the paper around the needle and attach the other end to a second needle.

4 Write something important or secret on the paper. Now roll up your scroll and tie a ribbon around it.

GOD'S SECRETARIES

The profession of scribe or secretary has been an important one throughout recorded history. In earliest times, scribes were the only people able to write and read.

The scribes often had top jobs at court, looking after the public records needed for government, and were highly respected.

Later, more people learned to read and write but scribes were still needed to do most of the written work.

The discovery of the Dead Sea Scrolls has shown how remarkably accurate the scribes' work was, with very few changes over a period of a thousand years or more. God's Law and the record of his relationship with his people has been accurately handed down to us, thanks to the work of the scribes.

IT'S A SCRIBE'S LIFE

A scribe was an important person in any town. He acted almost like our solicitors and lawyers do today. He had an 'office' near the town gate, where all business transactions were carried out. He could be hired to draw up a legal document, or make a will. If someone needed an important letter written, he would write and send it.

Other scribes had government jobs. They made lists and kept records, prepared accounts and worked on census and tax collection. High-ranking officials employed scribes as permanent secretaries.

Another important function was manuscript copying. Making copies of the scriptures, in particular, was considered a sacred task. There were very strict rules about how it should be done, and the scribes took great care to avoid making any mistakes. There were several checks to help them. The scribe would count the number of lines and compare them with the original. He would note any damage to the original.

Words of Jesus:
'Till heaven and earth pass away, not one jot, not one tittle, will pass from the law, until all is accomplished.'
MATTHEW 5:18

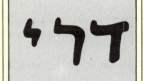

A 'jot' ('y') was the smallest letter in the Hebrew alphabet. A 'tittle' is the tiny mark which makes the letters 'd' and 'r' different from one another in Hebrew.

Sometimes a second scribe would check the whole copy.

Can I try the ancient art of copying?

Yes, but not on my answers!

THE DEAD SEA SCROLLS

DISCOVERY OF A LIFETIME!

The caves in the hills where the scrolls were found, seen from the air.

One winter afternoon in 1946–7, a lucky accident brought about a most important discovery. A shepherd watching his sheep on the hillsides close to the Dead Sea spotted a hole in the cliff face. He threw a stone inside and it made a strange noise. Exploring, he found a cave containing several jars about two feet tall. Inside two of them were leather scrolls wrapped in linen cloth.

Muhammed did not know what·to make of them. At first no one was interested. But when they reached the archaeologists there was great excitement. Eventually, fragments of about 400 scrolls were recovered and the shepherd's tribe became rich.

Secret community

The scrolls were the library of a Jewish religious community living on the shores of the Dead Sea at about the time when Jesus was alive. When the Roman army marched into Palestine in AD 68, no Jewish group was safe. Hastily they packed away their precious manuscripts in storage jars and, climbing the heights behind their headquarters, they hid them in some of the natural caves in the hillside.

New light on the scriptures

There were copies of every one of the Old Testament books except Esther, a thousand years earlier than any known before the find. They show remarkably few changes over that period of time and demonstrate the accuracy of the scribes who copied them.

There were also books on the Qumran community itself. They throw light on the way very strict religious Jews thought and lived at the time.

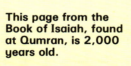

This page from the Book of Isaiah, found at Qumran, is 2,000 years old.

THE OLD TESTAMENT

It is not easy to discover exactly how the books of the Old Testament came to be written and collected together because many of them are so very old. They would have been passed on by word of mouth long before they were written down.

1 From earliest times, important things have been written down and kept in special places. In the book of Genesis it says: 'God said to Moses, write this on a scroll as something to be remembered . . .'

3 From the time of Samuel, the words and writings of the prophets were recorded and kept for future generations. For example, we know that Samuel's message about Israel's kings was kept in the sanctuary at Mizpeh.

2 Moses wrote down God's instructions in 'The Book of the Law'. It was then given to the priests to keep beside the covenant box or 'ark' in the sacred inner room of the tabernacle. The Ten Commandments would have been carved on stone tablets not more than 45 × 30cm. They were kept inside the covenant box.

THE APOCRYPHA

The name, which means 'hidden', applies to twelve books and additions to books which are very old and were included with other Old Testament books in the Greek translation, the Septuagint.

However, they were not included in the final list agreed at the Synod of Jamnia. Today they are included in Roman Catholic Bibles, though not usually in Protestant Bibles.

4 The collections of poems and songs in the book of Psalms was probably begun by David for use in the temple worship. Others would have been added to his collection over the years.

5 By the time of Ezra and Nehemiah, in the fifth century BC, the Pentateuch was complete and its authority recognized. Nehemiah is said to have founded 'a library, gathered together the books about the kings and prophets, and the books of David, and letters of kings about sacred gifts'.

7 By the time of Jesus all of the Old Testament books were well known and accepted. They were finally agreed at the Jewish Synod of Jamnia in AD 90. The Hebrew Bible used today contains all the Old Testament books in the Christian Bible, but some are in a different order.

6 In the time between the Old and New Testaments, a Jewish military leader named Judas Maccabaeus '. . . collected all the books that had been lost on account of the war . . .' It is most likely that he also arranged the complete collection, divided into three: the 'Law', the 'Prophets' and the rest.

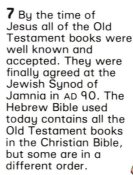

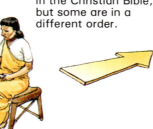

THE NEW TESTAMENT

There is much more evidence to go on when we come to the collection of the New Testament. Thousands of manuscripts (some going back to the early centuries AD) have been preserved and from them we can piece together what must have happened.

1 When the first Christian groups met together for worship, they continued to read the Jewish Old Testament, as Jesus had done. As well as this, people who had known Jesus were asked to talk about him and to share his teachings.

3 As time passed and eye-witnesses gradually died, the Christians realized that clear accounts of Jesus' life and work must be written down. This led Matthew and John, Mark (working with Peter) and Doctor Luke (journeying with Paul), to write down their Gospels. As the early church grew, Luke added the Acts of the Apostles to his Gospel.

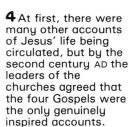

2 The first written documents circulating amongst the churches were the letters written by Paul. These were read and treasured by the people they were written to, and they were also copied and distributed to other churches nearby.

4 At first, there were many other accounts of Jesus' life being circulated, but by the second century AD the leaders of the churches agreed that the four Gospels were the only genuinely inspired accounts.

5 John's moving account of his visions about the end of time, called the Book of Revelation, was then added to the accepted documents. 2 Peter, 2 and 3 John, James, Jude and Hebrews were also accepted, after some debate, probably about their suitability for reading aloud in church.

6 The list of books as we now have it was agreed and in use long before the Councils of Laodicea (AD 363) and of Carthage (AD 397) formally accepted them. In making their final decisions, the Church Fathers asked themselves two questions: 'Does this book teach what the eye-witnesses, particularly the disciples of Jesus, taught?' and 'Does it encourage and strengthen Christians in their faith?'

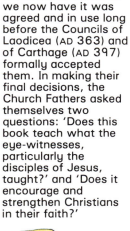

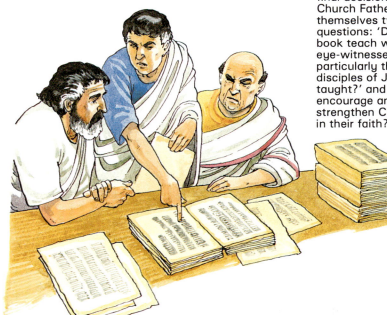

SPREADING THE WORD: A BIRD'S EYE VIEW

Almost before the final text of the Old and New Testaments had been agreed, there were moves to translate it into other languages. Over the centuries since, this desire to see the scriptures in the language of the different peoples has been given high priority by Christians. It is an exciting adventure story!

This chart shows the various translations from the beginning to the present day. It can be used as a reference for the following pages, or you can come back to it later.

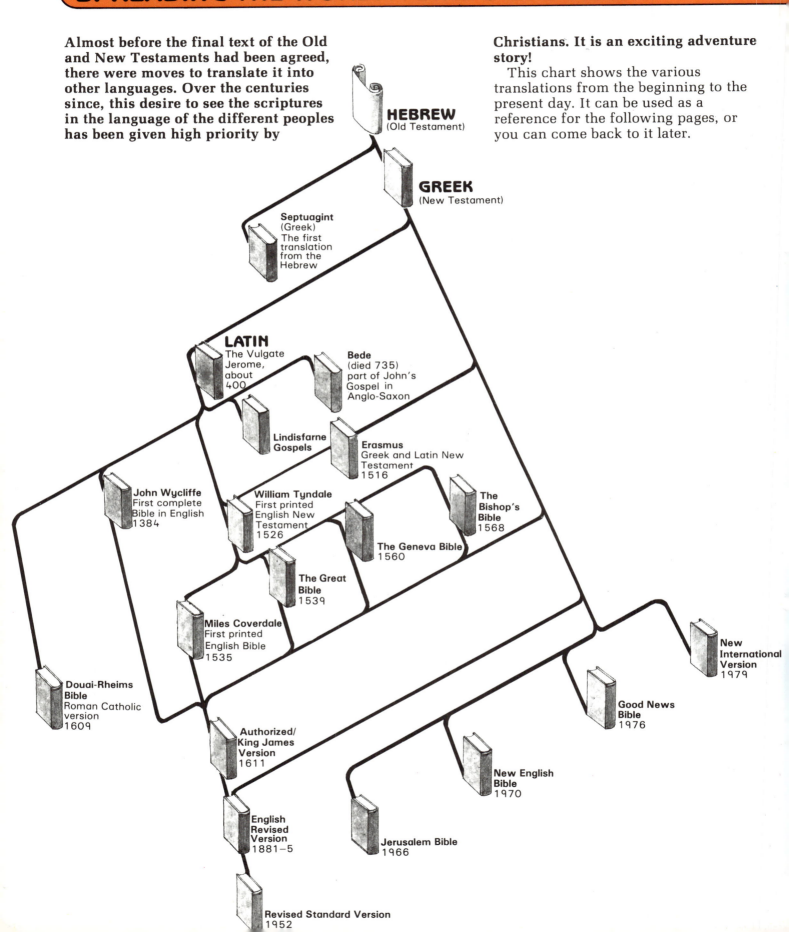

HEBREW (Old Testament)

GREEK (New Testament)

Septuagint (Greek) The first translation from the Hebrew

LATIN The Vulgate Jerome, about 400

Bede (died 735) part of John's Gospel in Anglo-Saxon

Lindisfarne Gospels

Erasmus Greek and Latin New Testament 1516

John Wycliffe First complete Bible in English 1384

William Tyndale First printed English New Testament 1526

The Bishop's Bible 1568

The Geneva Bible 1560

The Great Bible 1539

Miles Coverdale First printed English Bible 1535

New International Version 1979

Douai-Rheims Bible Roman Catholic version 1609

Good News Bible 1976

Authorized/ King James Version 1611

New English Bible 1970

English Revised Version 1881–5

Jerusalem Bible 1966

Revised Standard Version 1952

THE EARLIEST TRANSLATIONS

Jesus was born at a very remarkable time in world history. The Roman Empire had spread over a vast area around the Mediterranean, bringing political stability. Greek ('Hellenistic') culture had brought a common language to the whole region. Ideas could circulate freely. It was into this world that the early Christians began to preach and to plant churches.

Originally in Greek, the common language of the people, the New Testament was soon translated into Latin, the official language of the Roman Empire. But there were soon too many versions and Pope Damasus commissioned his secretary, Jerome, to make an authorized version. This was completed in about AD 400 and became known as the Vulgate, which means 'common' or 'popular'.

Jerome (Eusebius Hieronymus), born in Italy about AD 345, is the most famous early Bible translator. He was a brilliant linguist and instead of simply revising the Latin text, he went back to the original Greek and Hebrew (with the help of a Jewish Rabbi) to produce a brand new version. It took him twenty-one years to complete! Many people disliked the new version at first, but it became the standard Bible of the Roman Catholic church and scores of other translations have been made from it.

1

Syriac
By AD 100 the Old Testament had already been translated into Syriac, the language of the people based around Edessa in modern Turkey, and by AD 400 Bishop Rabbula of Edessa had produced the whole Bible. It was called the Peshitta or 'simple' version.

Missionaries from the Syriac church went as far afield as India and China. There is evidence of the Gospel of Matthew in Syriac being used in India in AD 180.

2

Coptic
The early Christians in Egypt spoke Coptic, a form of ancient Egyptian. The Bible was first translated into the Sahidic dialect of the south and later into other dialects of Egypt. No one speaks Coptic today but it is still used as the language of the church of Egypt.

3

Armenian and Georgian
Syriac missionaries went north into Armenia (now part of the USSR). Part of the Bible was translated into Armenian as early as the fifth century.

The Armenians then evangelized the Georgians, to the north, making a translation of their own Bible into the Georgian language.

4

Germanic
The Ostragoths of northern Europe were called 'barbarians' by the Romans, but they became Christians as early as the third century. Their Bishop, Ulfilas, made a translation of the Bible in the middle of the fourth century. A famous copy, now in Sweden, was written in silver and gold on purple vellum.

5

Old Slavonic
In the ninth century AD two brothers, Cyril and Methodius, went as missionaries to the Slavic Empire. In order to write down their Bible, the brothers invented an alphabet for the Slavs. It is called the Cyrillic alphabet, and is still used in Eastern Europe and Russia today.

MONKS AND MANUSCRIPTS

Throughout the period we call the Dark Ages (because we have so little information about what was going on), the Latin Vulgate was the only Bible used in Europe. But soon after the break-up of the Roman Empire, Latin ceased to be the language spoken or even understood by ordinary people.

For some 900 years the Bible was therefore in the hands of church leaders and monks, not read by the people. So medieval Christians depended for their knowledge of Bible stories on what they could see in their local church. Art and drama became very important to them.

Mystery plays

Mystery plays began in church as dramatic readings of parts of the Bible used in the Mass. As they became more elaborate, the plays were moved outside, onto the church steps, and then to other public places. Eventually they included many biblical scenes, teaching the whole story from the Garden of Eden to the Day of Judgment.

Manuscripts

Because they took so long to copy by hand, Bibles were very precious. The monks who made them their life's work took great pains to make them as beautiful as possible, decorating the pages and 'illuminating' them with gold leaf.

Stained glass

The art of stained glass, painting and sculpture were all used to decorate churches, but more importantly to teach people basic Bible truths.

This is the beautiful rose window from Notre Dame, in Paris.

Its stained glass panels tell a whole series of Bible stories in pictures.

MAKE YOUR OWN DECORATED PSALM

Try your hand at making a beautiful copy of Psalm 23. You could hang it on your wall, or give it to someone as a gift.

1 On a piece of tracing-paper, copy the capital 'T' on this page.

2 Transfer this to a piece of good card, going over your pencil lines in ink.

3 Now write in the rest of the psalm. If you can use an italic pen, it will look good.

4 Colour in your work. Add small decorations like the ones shown here.

THE EARLY ENGLISH BIBLE

The earliest translation in England was made by **Aldhelm**, Bishop of Sherborne in Dorset, soon after AD 700.

●At about the same time, in the north of England, the monk and historian **Bede** began to translate the Gospel of John into Anglo-Saxon, so that English Christians could have some of the Bible in their very own language.

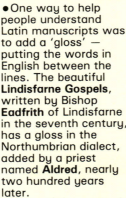

●The English **King Alfred** (AD 871–901) was unusually well-educated for kings of the period, and eager to help his subjects. He translated parts of Exodus, Psalms and Acts.

●One way to help people understand Latin manuscripts was to add a 'gloss' — putting the words in English between the lines. The beautiful **Lindisfarne Gospels**, written by Bishop **Eadfrith** of Lindisfarne in the seventh century, has a gloss in the Northumbrian dialect, added by a priest named **Aldred**, nearly two hundred years later.

●None of the work of Bede, Aldhelm or Alfred has survived. The earliest English versions still existing are the **Wessex Gospels**, and the first seven books of the Old Testament by **Abbot Aelfric** of Eynsham in the tenth century.

●After the Norman conquest of 1066, some educated priests made their own translations into various local dialects.

●One Augustinian monk named **Orm** produced a version of the Gospels and Acts in verse. One copy of this work from the thirteenth century has survived. It is called the **Ormulum**.

●Although most of these were translations into English dialects, they did not reach the ordinary person. The people of England had to wait for a man named **Wycliffe** in the fourteenth century before there was any real move to create a Bible they could understand.

REVOLUTIONARY TIMES

Towards the end of the Middle Ages, the church had become very corrupt. Popes had become rich and powerful rulers. Many priests were ignorant and greedy and some were living openly immoral lives.

As a result, individuals and groups of Christians all over Europe began to speak out against the state of the church and to meet to worship independently. Protest was a dangerous business, but many brave men were willing to risk their lives, especially to bring the Bible — the word of God — to ordinary people in their own language.

In England many read John Wycliffe's Bible in secret. Each handwritten copy took about ten months and cost £40 to produce. Some of Wycliffe's followers were burned, with their Bibles around their necks.

WANTED

JAN HUS

This man is Rector of the University of Prague, Bohemia (Czechoslovakia). He has been reading the Bible for himself, and trying to introduce New Testament practices, so creating civil unrest. He is wanted to appear before the Council of Constance.

1414

Wanted

PETER WALDO

A wealthy merchant of Lyons, France, and leader of the group known as the Poor Men of Lyons, or Waldensians

This group live a life of simple poverty and good works. But they preach to the poor from the Bible, turning the people against the clergy. By arranging for the Bible to be translated into Provençal, Waldo has made it possible for anyone in southern France to read the Bible for himself and interpret it how he will. These people must be stopped! All Waldensians are declared excommunicated by order of Pope Lucius III.

1184

WANTED

John Wycliffe

John Wycliffe, Oxford theologian, has taken it into his own hands to commission a translation of the Latin Vulgate Bible into English. The work has been carried out by scholars Nicholas of Hereford and John Purvey. It is being distributed by Wycliffe's followers, known as the Lollards. These cranks and mumblers are teaching against the practices of the church and must be suppressed.

A synod of the church has now met in Oxford, and the writing, circulation and study of these English versions of the Bible is officially banned.

1408

PRINTERS AT WORK

While Europe was in the midst of religious and political turmoil, there was another revolution going on. This mechanical invention, the printing press, was to speed up the changes happening everywhere.

In the city of Mainz, Germany, Johann Gutenberg was experimenting with movable metal type for printing books. Handcut wooden blocks for printing had been invented in Asia in about the fifth century AD and the first known printed book was produced by this means in China in 868. Gutenberg simply took the block idea and simplified it, so that individual letters could be made up into words and lines and assembled to form a page, which could

then be mounted on a simple press.

Now a positive flood of books could be produced quickly and at relatively low cost. This was the big moment! The age of print had arrived. And it was just in time for the Reformers, ready with their new translations of the Bible. Up until then, every copy had been produced by hand. Now printing was seen as the way to get copies of scripture into the hands of ordinary people. The very first complete book known

to have been printed in the western world was the Bible, in 1456.

Until 1462 the new art remained a closely guarded trade secret in Mainz, but in that year

the city was plundered and the printers scattered. Within 20 years, the invention had spread far and wide, with presses in Rome, Paris, Cracow and London. In 1476 William Caxton set up his printing-press at the sign of the Red Pale in the Almonry at Westminster (modern Tothill Street).

The picture shows a reconstruction of the room in which Gutenberg printed his first books.

MAKE YOUR OWN PRINTING-BLOCK

1 Write your name on a piece of tracing-paper. Turn it over and trace your name backwards onto a small block of wood.

2 Glue some light string along the pencil lines.

3 Press your 'printing block' onto an office ink-pad.

4 Now you can print your name, on letters or in your own books.

AN EXPLOSION OF TRANSLATIONS

Four major developments in the middle of the fifteenth century contributed to the sudden flood of new Bible translations in Europe. The first was printing, which revolutionized the spread of ideas.

The second was the fall of Constantinople, capital of the eastern Roman Empire, to the Turks in 1453. Many Greek scholars fled from the city, taking their priceless manuscripts with them. As they settled in the West, they contributed a much deeper knowledge of the Greek New Testament to the men working on the new translations.

This event also contributed to the third development, the remarkable revival of learning, known as the Renaissance. This created an openness to new ideas in science, art and the study of the classics. The cobwebs of medieval scholarship were being blown away. People were open to change, to radical new ideas.

The fourth development, as a result of having the Bible widely available, was a rediscovery of the message of the gospel. Men such as Luther, Erasmus, Calvin and Knox were able to point to the scriptures and challenge the practices of the church. The Reformation had begun.

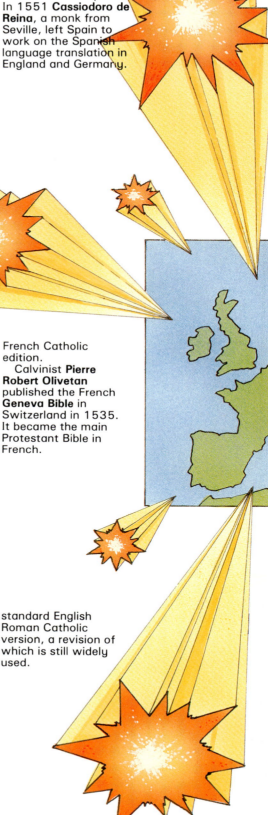

Spanish

All Bible translation was banned in Spain. In 1551 **Cassiodoro de Reina**, a monk from Seville, left Spain to work on the Spanish language translation in England and Germany.

French

In France, the work of translation was begun by a Roman Catholic priest, **Jacques Lefèvre d'Etaples**. He published his Bible in Belgium because the French authorities were suspicious of his sympathy with the Reformation movement. It was banned by the church and a new translation commissioned from scholars at Louvain University. This has become the standard French Catholic edition.

Calvinist **Pierre Robert Olivetan** published the French **Geneva Bible** in Switzerland in 1535. It became the main Protestant Bible in French.

English

Bible translation in England was still banned when Oxford scholar **William Tyndale** set out to make a new translation, working from the original Hebrew and Erasmus's Greek. 'A boy who drives the plough in England,' Tyndale prophesied, 'shall know more of the Bible than many priests.'

Fierce opposition forced him to travel to Germany to finish the New Testament, which was published at Worms in 1525. Copies printed in Germany were smuggled into England, where King Henry VIII ordered them to be burned!

While Tyndale was working on the Old Testament, he was betrayed, arrested and burned at the stake. 'Lord, open the King of England's eyes,' he prayed. And when the first complete Bible was printed in England it had King Henry VIII's blessing.

The Authorized, King James Version, 1611, closely follows Tyndale's New Testament.

In 1609, **Gregory Martin**, in exile at the Roman Catholic English College at Douay in France, published the **Douai-Rheims Bible**, the standard English Roman Catholic version, a revision of which is still widely used.

Swedish
By 1541 Sweden had a standard translation in the **Uppsala Bible**, made by Laurentius Petri, Archbishop of Uppsala.

Danish
In Denmark, the standard version was the **King Christian III Bible** printed in 1550 in Copenhagen.

Dutch
The earliest Dutch Bible was the **Mennonite** version of 1558. Calvinists used the Statenvertaling edition produced at the expense of the Dutch states.
  Nicholas van Winghe made the Catholic translation from the Vulgate in 1548.

German
Martin Luther was a German monk. The son of a miner, he became a Professor at Wittenberg University in 1511. Deeply concerned at his own spiritual state, he studied the scriptures.

Reading Paul's letter to the Romans, he found that his salvation depended not on his own efforts to be good but on what Jesus had done for him.
  He denounced the wrong practices of the church of his time and was exiled to the Wartburg castle. There he began his translation, which has been the standard German Protestant Bible ever since.

Italian
The greatest Italian version was made by **Giovanni Diodati** in Geneva in 1607.

Greek
Born in Rotterdam Holland, in 1466, **Desiderius Erasmus** became one of the greatest Renaissance linguists and scholars. In 1516 he produced the first published Greek New Testament.

THE ENGLISH BIBLE: WYCLIFFE TO KING JAMES

Just as the translation and distribution of the Bible was being undertaken all over Europe, so in England the movement took off.

After William Tyndale, there followed a century of feverish activity, culminating in the Authorized or King James Version in 1611.

But translators had to be careful. They were engaged on a dangerous business; the ban on English scriptures was severe. Many of them had to remain in exile on the continent, arranging for their Bibles to be smuggled into the country by sympathetic merchants. But neither burning books nor killing the translators could stop the movement that brought the Bible to ordinary people in their own language.

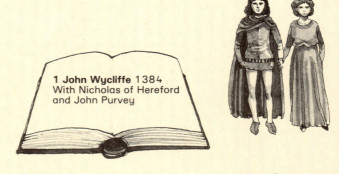

1 John Wycliffe 1384
With Nicholas of Hereford and John Purvey

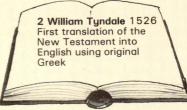

2 William Tyndale 1526
First translation of the New Testament into English using original Greek

3 Miles Coverdale 1535
First complete printed Bible in English

HOW LANGUAGE CHANGES

Here are the first few lines of Psalm 23 in some of the historic English versions. They show the language changing over 200 years. It is interesting to compare them with modern versions.

Wycliffe Bible
The Lord gouerneth me, and no thing to me shal lacke; in the place of leswe where he me ful sette. Ouer watir of fulfilling he nurshide me; my soule he conuertide.

Coverdale Bible
The Lorde is my shepherde, I can wante nothinge. He fedeth me in a grene pasture, and ledeth ne to a fresh water. He quickeneth my soule . . .

Bishops' Bible
God is my sheephearde, therfore I can lacke nothyng: he wyll cause me to repose my selfe in pasture full of grasse, and he wyll leade me unto calme waters. He wyll conuert my soule . . .

Douai
Our Lord ruleth me, and nothing shal be wanting to me: in place of pasture there he hath placed me. Upon the water of refection he hath brought me up: he hath conuerted my soule.

Authorized/King James Version
The Lord is my shepherd; I shall not want. He maketh me to lie down in green pastures: he leadeth me beside the still waters. He restoreth my soul.

By 1538 so much had changed in England that the Bible in English could be used publicly in every church. Bibles were so valuable, however, that they were chained to a desk to deter thieves.

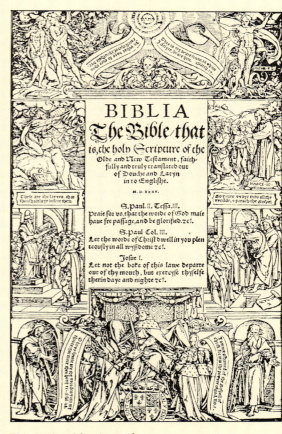

This is the title page of the first Bible to be printed in English: Miles Coverdale's translation, 1535.

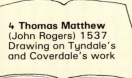

4 Thomas Matthew
(John Rogers) 1537
Drawing on Tyndale's and Coverdale's work

5 Great Bible 1539
Coverdale's revision of Matthew's Bible authorized by Henry VIII for use in churches

6 Geneva Bible 1560
Revision of Great Bible by William Whittingham and others in exile in Geneva, the **'Breeches' Bible**

7 Bishops' Bible 1568
Revision of the Great Bible by a group of bishops and scholars under Matthew Parker, Archbishop of Canterbury

8 Rheims New Testament 1582
Gregory Martin and others in exile from Oxford worked on the Roman Catholic English translation

9 Douai Old Testament 1609
The same group completed the Old Testament, the college having moved to Douai

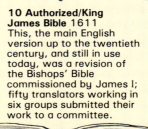

10 Authorized/King James Bible 1611
This, the main English version up to the twentieth century, and still in use today, was a revision of the Bishops' Bible commissioned by James I; fifty translators working in six groups submitted their work to a committee.

TO THE ENDS OF THE EARTH

The changes brought about by the Reformation were so important and far reaching that the Protestant churches spent the next century or more sorting out their own patterns of worship and belief. The Roman Catholic Church meantime (especially the Jesuits, founded in 1540) was sending missionaries as far afield as India, Indonesia and Japan, China, Mexico, Brazil and Paraguay.

In an effort to bring Catholic missions under Vatican control, Pope Gregory XV founded the Sacred Congregation for the Propagation of the Faith, known as Propaganda. Its missionaries were courageous in founding churches and translating parts of the Bible for the people. They usually began with the Ten Commandments, the Lord's Prayer and selected parts of the Gospels, or with Bible story books, as well as the catechism. In 1613 Jesuit missionaries published the whole New Testament in Japanese.

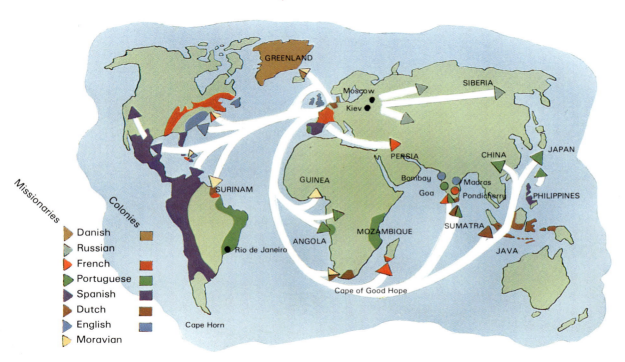

Missionaries

Colonies

Danish	
Russian	
French	
Portuguese	
Spanish	
Dutch	
English	
Moravian	

TRADERS AND MISSIONARIES

The story of Protestant missionary work (and Catholic too) goes hand in hand with the exploration and colonization of the world outside Europe in the seventeenth century. A hundred years after pioneer explorers such as Columbus and da Gama opened up the world, the era of foreign conquest and trade was in full swing.

With the trading companies went chaplains whose job was not only to look after the company workers but also to evangelize the local people. In this way, for example, Protestant missionaries from England, Germany, Holland, Moravia and Denmark established work in India, Sri Lanka, Malaya, South Africa and New England.

Exciting reports of work with the American Indians reached Britain. Christians were keen to offer help and support and the New England Company was formed in 1649, becoming, in effect, the first missionary society.

In the following 300 years, a number of missionary societies were set up. By the end of the nineteenth century they were sending Christian missionaries to preach and teach and heal all over the world.

The Massachusetts Bible

At the beginning of the seventeenth century the non-conformists known as Puritans were so persecuted in England that a group of them set sail in *The Mayflower* to begin a new life in America. In Boston, John Eliot began to work with the Massachusetts Indians and by 1663 he had translated the whole Bible into their language.

Malay and Tamil

The Dutch and the Danes were busy traders in the East Indies, and the earliest Malay Gospel translations were the work of a Dutch East Indies Company director.

One of the best-known translations of the seventeenth century is Danish missionary Bartholomaus Ziegenbalg's Tamil New Testament. It was the first Bible in an Indian language.

THE BIBLE SOCIETIES

Sometimes great movements can be sparked off by what seem like very small events.

Mary Jones

Mary Jones was a poor Welsh girl, about eight years old. She loved to hear stories from the Bible and longed to read them for herself. But no one in the family could read, and Bibles in the Welsh language were rare and expensive. When Mary was ten she was able to walk the two miles to school and learned to read. She determined to save up for a Bible of her own. It took her six long years.

When at last she had enough money for the precious book, she walked the twenty-five miles to the town of Bala, barefoot.

Faint with exhaustion, Mary asked the Rev. Thomas Charles if she could buy a Bible. He had three left, all of them promised to other buyers. But he was so sorry for Mary that he let her have one.

We would never have heard this story, except for the fact that Thomas Charles was asked to speak at a meeting of the Religious Tract Society about the need of Bibles in Welsh.

Mary's story, and many others from different parts of the world, so moved the people present that, in 1804, the British and Foreign Bible Society was formed. Its aim was to provide Bibles for as many people as possible, in their own languages and at a price they could afford.

Following the lead of the British and Foreign Bible Society, other Bible Societies were formed, beginning in Glasgow in 1805, until the movement had spread throughout Europe and the British Empire. By 1907 there were some 8,700 branch societies and auxiliaries — and a staggering 203,931,768 Bibles, Testaments and portions of Scripture had been put into circulation.

UNITED BIBLE SOCIETIES

In 150 years the Bible Society movement had grown so large that in 1946 a co-operative organization was formed. It had six main purposes.

● To encourage co-operation between the societies.
● To exchange information and harmonize policies and techniques worldwide.
● To supply members with help and services.
● To collect information on religious trends in the world as they affect the Bible.

● To represent the Bible Societies in talks with other Christian organizations.
● To supply emergency services anywhere in the world.

UBS regional offices were set up in Nairobi, Mexico City, Singapore and Brussels. Each office has specialists in Bible translation, production and distribution. The world UBS translation co-ordinator supervises 50 translations consultants. During the 1970s, these consultants were involved in over 800 different translation projects at one time.

BIBLE SOCIETIES GROW

- 1804 British and Foreign
- 1805 Glasgow
- 1806 Hibernian (Irish)
- 1807 Canadian
- 1809 Edinburgh committee
- 1813 Russian
- 1814 Danish
- 1814 Dutch
- 1815 Swedish
- 1816 American
- 1816 Norwegian
- 1817 Australian
- 1836 Baptists form the American and Foreign
- 1837 New Zealand
- 1946 Polish
- 1946 United Bible Societies formed
- 1948 German

1800 1820 1840 1860 1880 1900 1920 1940 1960

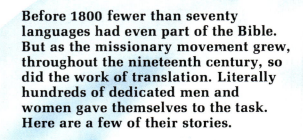

TRANSLATORS' TALES

Before 1800 fewer than seventy languages had even part of the Bible. But as the missionary movement grew, throughout the nineteenth century, so did the work of translation. Literally hundreds of dedicated men and women gave themselves to the task. Here are a few of their stories.

A SHOEMAKER GOES TO INDIA

William Carey was an apprentice shoemaker in Northamptonshire, England, when he became a Christian through the influence of a fellow apprentice. He became a Baptist minister and taught himself Latin, Greek, Hebrew, French and Dutch. He helped to found the Baptist Missionary Society and, as one of its first missionaries, set off for Bengal in India in 1793.

For the next thirty years Carey put all his efforts into founding churches and training Indian Christian leaders. He helped the Indian people through such practical projects as schools, hospitals and agricultural reform, and worked towards the abolition of 'sati' (the practice of burning a man's widow at his death).

Carey and his colleagues also set up a printing press and translated portions of the Bible into forty-five languages and dialects. Carey himself learned Sanskrit, Bengali, Marathi and Sinhalese. His dream was that all the peoples of the East should have a Bible they could read.

কারণ ঈশ্বর জগৎকে এমন প্রেম করিলেন যে, আপনার একজাত পুত্রকে দান করিলেন, যেন, যে কেহ তাঁহাতে বিশ্বাস করে, সে বিনষ্ট না হয়, কিন্তু অনন্ত জীবন পায়।

John 3:16 in Bengali

RISKING DEATH IN CHINA

In the nineteenth century China was completely closed to the West. Nothing had been done to take the Christian message to its people since the arrival of Roman Catholic missionaries three centuries earlier.

Joshua Marshman, a colleague of William Carey in India, felt strongly that the Bible should be translated into Chinese. With the help of John Lassar, an Armenian who had been born in Macao in China, he began work, and the whole Bible was finished by 1822.

At the same time, another man was translating the Bible in China itself. Robert Morrison was determined to study the language. It was virtually unknown in England and he used a copy of part of the New Testament in Chinese made by an eighteenth-century Jesuit missionary, which he found in the British Museum, London.

Morrison was not allowed to travel further than the trading-post in Canton

生。滅亡，反得永 信他的，叫一切 他們，叫一切不至 獨生子賜給他的， 甚至將他的 上帝愛世人，

John 3:16 in Kuoyu Chinese

where he was the official interpreter for his company. Undeterred, he found a local Chinese teacher. It was so dangerous to be discovered teaching a foreigner Chinese that his teacher always carried poison, ready to take if he was caught.

Another missionary, William Milne, joined Morrison in 1817 and in 1823 their complete Bible was published. Robert Morrison died alone in Canton, only eight years before missionaries were at last allowed in China. His work formed the basis for their evangelism.

BIBLES FOR COCONUT OIL

The languages of India and China had been written down for centuries, but elsewhere in the world there were still many thousands of peoples with no written language at all.

When William Ellis went to the Pacific island of Tahiti for the London Missionary Society in 1817 he realized that he must start from scratch, learning the language, deciding which letters should be used for the sounds and how words should be spelled. His first book in Tahitian was a small spelling manual. The king of Tahiti was so eager to see how the language of his people would look on paper that he pulled the first pages off the printing press himself.

With the king's help, some parts of the Bible soon followed. The people of Tahiti were so eager to buy them that those with no money were allowed to pay in coconut oil. Three gallons bought a copy of St Luke's Gospel!

John 3:16 in Tahitian

I aroha mai te Atua i to te ao, e ua tae roa i te horoa mai i ta 'na Tamaiti fanau tahi, ia ore ia pohe te faaroo ia 'na ra, ia roaa râ te ora mure ore.

FROM PADDINGTON TO PERU

The first printed scripture in a South American language came about in a very unusual way. James Thomson, a missionary on leave, met a man on a bus in Paddington, London. The man turned out to be Vincente Pazos-Kanki, a professor from Cuzco in Peru. His mother was an Indian of the Aymara tribe, an advanced civilization before their conquest by the Incas. James Thomson persuaded Dr Pazos-Kanki to translate Luke's Gospel for the Aymara people.

Cunalaycutejja Diosaji uqhama acapacharu muni, jupa sapa jathata Yokaparu churi, take qhititi juparu iyausisqui ucajja, jan chhakhtasiñapataqui, ucatsipana wiñaya jacañaniñapataqui.

John 3:16 in Aymara

THE SLAVE WHO BECAME A BISHOP

In 1821 an eleven-year-old Yoruba boy called Adjai, with his mother and two sisters, was kidnapped by slave traders in West Africa. Separated from his family, Adjai was taken to Lagos, Nigeria, where he was bought and sold several times. His fifth master sold him onto a Portuguese slave-ship. One day out of Lagos, however, a British warship intercepted the slaver and took the freed slaves to Sierra Leone.

Once there, Adjai was able to go to a Christian school, where he proved to be very intelligent and quick to learn. He was baptized in 1825, taking the name Samuel Crowther. He was later ordained in London and became the first African bishop.

Among the first people to become Christians when he returned to his own Yoruba people were his long-lost mother and sister. In Nigeria he appointed an all-African staff, believing that the evangelization of inland Africa must be carried out by Africans. He also set up a joint team of Europeans and his own people to translate the Bible into Yoruba. It was finished in 1884.

INTO EVERY LANGUAGE

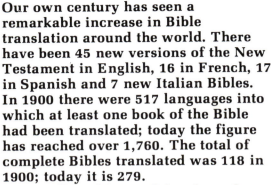

Our own century has seen a remarkable increase in Bible translation around the world. There have been 45 new versions of the New Testament in English, 16 in French, 17 in Spanish and 7 new Italian Bibles. In 1900 there were 517 languages into which at least one book of the Bible had been translated; today the figure has reached over 1,760. The total of complete Bibles translated was 118 in 1900; today it is 279.

As well as this, work has been done on some 800 out of an estimated 3–4,000 new or unwritten languages around the world.

WYCLIFFE BIBLE TRANSLATORS

A young American missionary was selling Spanish Bibles in Guatemala when an Indian asked him, 'Why, if your God is so smart, doesn't he speak my language?'

Immediately William Cameron Townsend set about seeing what could be done to show the Indian that God did understand his language. He began translating the New Testament into Cakchiquel. It took him fifteen years.

By now Townsend realized the need for Bibles in many other languages. His work led to the founding of the Wycliffe Bible Translators in 1934.

THE ENGLISH BIBLE FOR THE MODERN WORLD

The Authorized or King James Version of the Bible was translated over 350 years ago. The Revised Version in the last century kept the same language but made revisions in the light of new work on the original Hebrew and Greek texts.

Since then, there have been a number of translations and paraphrases designed to bring the Bible to a much wider readership in the modern world.

New translations were pioneered by the classical scholar, R. T. Weymouth (1903), J. Moffatt (1913 and 1924), the American translation of E. J. Goodspeed (1927) and the Roman Catholic translation from the Vulgate by Ronald Knox (1944 and 1949).

A key post-war translation was *The New Testament in Modern English* by J. B. Phillips, a fresh, free translation. Since then there has been a succession of new versions, notably:

Revised Standard Version
A revision of the American Standard Version, which was itself a revision of the Authorized King James Version. 1946 and 1952

Schonfield
The Authentic New Testament by H. J. Schonfield, a distinguished Jewish scholar. 1955

The Amplified Bible
A version giving alternative words for different possible meanings. 1958

Berkeley
An American revision. 1959

At her coronation in 1953, Queen Elizabeth II was presented with a copy of the Bible with the words, '. . . we present you with this book, the most valuable thing that this world affords. Here is wisdom; this is the royal law; these are the lively oracles of God.'

Today it is the largest missionary society in the world, with over 3,000 workers.

Wycliffe Bible Translators are at work in the following countries (the number in brackets shows how many languages or dialects they are working on):

Africa (in addition to individual countries listed) (53)
Asia (63)
Australia (25)
Bolivia (19)
Brazil (48)
Cameroon/Chad (38)
Colombia (37)
Ecuador (13)
Europe (3)
Ghana (18)

Guatemala/Honduras (38)
Indonesia (24)
Ivory Coast/Upper Volta (24)
Latin America (in addition to countries listed) (10)
Malaysia (3)
Mali (30)
Mexico (137)

Papua New Guinea (152)
Peru/Chile (51)
Philippines (68)
Solomon Islands (14)
Sudan (15)
Surinam (7)
Togo/Benin (7)
USA/Canada (55)

New English Bible
A completely new, formal translation sponsored by the main British churches and Bible Societies. 1961 and 1970

New American Standard Version
A revision of the American Revised. 1963

The Jerusalem Bible
The work of the Roman Catholic School of Biblical Studies, Jerusalem. 1966

Good News Bible
Known at first as *Today's English Version*, this was a completely new translation using English 'common' to people from many different backgrounds for whom English may be their first or second language. It was sponsored by the American Bible Society. 1966 and 1976

New American Bible
A Roman Catholic translation sponsored by the Bishops' Committee of the Confraternity of Christian doctrine. 1970

The Living Bible
A paraphrase for family reading by Kenneth Taylor. 1971

New International Version
A new translation by a team of international scholars. 1972 and 1979

The Common Bible
The American Revised Standard Version with the addition of the Apocrypha. 1973

Revised Authorized Version
An updating of the original Authorized King James Version. 1982

LANGUAGES STILL NEEDING TRANSLATION

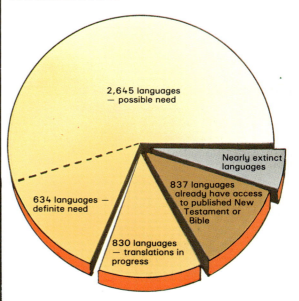

2,645 languages — possible need

634 languages — definite need

830 languages — translations in progress

837 languages already have access to published New Testament or Bible

Nearly extinct languages

FROM THE PEN TO THE PAGE

There are several ways in which translation work can be carried out. Where there is no established local church or group of believers, translators work with a national interpreter.

Increasingly, however, the local church starts off the process. One of its members, trained in linguistics, will take on the work, drawing on outside help from experts when necessary.

Today, too, the Bible Societies are working on different kinds of translation to meet specific needs: simple language editions for those just learning to read; and 'common' language versions for distribution to people with little knowledge of religious language or the background to the Bible.

FIRST STEPS

Unwritten languages

1 Learn the language with a local interpreter. Decide which letters from the Roman alphabet will stand for which sounds.

2 Produce an alphabet, grammar and complete list of words.

3 Teach people to read their language.

4 Translate portions of the Bible, from the Hebrew and Greek, into the local language.

5 Check with people at each stage, to make sure it conveys accurately the sense of the original.

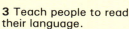

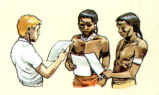

4 Bible Society adviser will keep in close touch with translation team, giving advice and help throughout the process.

Languages already written

1 A trained national gathers a local group to make first drafts. They discuss, correct and agree drafts.

2 Experts on the Bible and language check the drafts.

3 Local church leaders see drafts for their advice and approval.

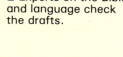

Once the basic translation has been made there is a constant need for revision. Living languages change so fast that each translation needs to be reviewed every thirty years. Many older versions need complete re-translation to take account of the new light shed upon the original texts by modern discoveries and scholarship.

Translation has always been a slow and painstaking process. Today we can take advantage of new technology, but the work is as exacting as ever. All over the world there are dedicated men and women, called by God to make sure that everyone can have the Bible in a language they really understand.

INTO PRINT

However a translation is made, the agreed text must undergo a long production process to turn it from manuscript or typescript into a printed book.

The typescript is first keyed into a computer typesetting machine, which reproduces the text on film.

Proof copies of the text are carefully checked for mistakes, and corrected.

From the film, plates are made which fit onto the cylinders of the printing machine.

Printed sections are gathered in the right order, glued into the cover, and trimmed to size.

Finished books can now be packed and delivered.

GUIDELINES FOR TRANSLATORS

The modern translator follows certain important rules and guidelines.
● Nothing must be added.
● Nothing must be left out.
● The original meaning must not be changed.

● Difficult ideas must be expressed in the closest *natural* equivalent of the original in the new language.

For example, in the Konkomba language of Ghana, the expression for being alive is 'to have a nose', so 'eternal life', literally translated back into English, reads: 'he should have nose which not has end'! If you think that sounds funny, how about 'pulling someone's leg'.

BE A TRANSLATOR

Read the first four sentences in Konkomba, a real language spoken in Ghana. Notice how the accent or tone marks make all the difference to the meaning (ú means the voice rises on that letter, ù means it falls). Now see if you can translate number 5, and write number 6 in Konkomba.

1 ù sú úpìì   He skinned a sheep.

2 ù sú ùpíí   He skinned a woman.

3 ù sù úpìì   He stole a sheep.

4 ù sù ùpíí   He stole a woman.

5 ùpíí sú úpìì   _____

6 _____ A woman stole a sheep.

WHAT'S SO SPECIAL ABOUT THE BIBLE?

The Bible makes important claims for itself. Here are some of them.

> **All Scripture is inspired by God and is useful for teaching the truth, rebuking error, correcting faults, and giving instruction for right living, so that the person who serves God may be fully qualified and equipped to do every kind of good deed.**
> 2 TIMOTHY 3:16

> **The word of God is alive and active, sharper than any double-edged sword. It cuts all the way through, to where soul and spirit meet, to where joints and marrow come together. It judges the desires and thoughts of man's heart.**
> HEBREWS 4:12

We have discovered a lot about the story of this remarkable book, the Bible, from earliest times to the efforts of thousands of people worldwide who have made it available to readers of every tribe and nation today. The Bible has changed millions of lives. It has revolutionized whole countries. What makes it so special?

The Bible is God's own story. If people want to know who God is, what he is like and what he has done, the Bible will tell them.

And what has God done? The Bible gives us the story of the people God chose for his own. It tells us of the life, teaching, death and resurrection of Jesus. It has a message for us today. It has answers to our deepest needs — forgiveness and a new start in life. It offers us hope and a real purpose.

In the introduction to his Gospel, Luke writes:

> **Your Excellency, because I have carefully studied all these matters from their beginning, I thought it would be good to write an orderly account for you. I do this so that you will know the full truth about everything which you have been taught.**
> LUKE 1:3–4

Jesus himself said:

> **Everything written about me in the Law of Moses, the writings of the prophets, and the Psalms had to come true.**
> LUKE 24:44

> **What the scripture says is true for ever.**
> JOHN 10:35

WHAT DOES IT SAY?

The first chapters of *Genesis* set the scene. All the important human questions are outlined here: the creation of the universe and of mankind; our relationship to our Creator, to each other, and to nature. The human pride which distorted all these relationships, the 'fall' into sin, and the judgement which follows is seen in *Genesis 3*.

Genesis 12 begins a theme which runs throughout the world's history. It is a story of people chosen by God to carry his message to the whole human race.

It begins with God's promise to Abraham, the covenant-agreement made with Abraham and through him to his grandson Jacob, who was renamed 'Israel'. His twelve sons became the fathers of the twelve tribes of Israel.

GOD'S WORD AND REAL PEOPLE

Lambert Dolphin
a physicist studying the earth's atmosphere, tells what happened to him after he became a Christian.

'The following days and weeks saw miracle after miracle of God's working in my life. The Bible is a supernatural book to me. Old problems and desires have faded away. For the first time, I feel complete as a human being.'

Vonda Kay Van Dyke
was a top model competing for the Miss America title. She faced a tough question from the judge:

'I understand you always carry a Bible with you. Do you consider your Bible a good luck charm?'

She replied: 'I do not consider my Bible a good luck charm, it is the most important book I own. My relationship with God is not as a religion but a faith.'

Kipchoge Keino
is a Kenyan, and the most successful runner Africa has ever produced. He remembers:

'My father-in-law used to read the Bible to me. He often explained difficult passages and many times we would discuss the Word of God late at night. The Bible convicted and convinced me of my need for salvation . . . As a runner I am training hard to win my races . . . but, win or lose, I know God is guiding me and has a purpose and plan for my life.'

Exodus tells us how God's people became slaves in Egypt, and about Moses, the man God sent to free them. God gave the people his Law, showing them how to live.

Joshua and *Judges* tell the story of how they settled in their new land, Canaan.

Ruth, Samuel, Kings, Chronicles, Ezra, Nehemiah and the *prophets* trace the long history of God's people to the end of the Old Testament. They have not lived up to God's law. They have been unfaithful to him. A new agreement must be made between God and mankind.

Jesus was the key to that agreement. Born in obscurity, he was gradually discovered by his followers to be the promised Messiah, the Son of God. His life was a perfect example of how we should live. And yet he was killed.

But his death turned out to be his greatest triumph. He was dying for the sins of the whole world. And after three days, he came to life again. His story is written in the Gospels of *Matthew, Mark, Luke* and *John* whose different accounts build up a full picture of Jesus the Messiah, the Christ.

Jesus expanded the dream of one nation into God's plan for the whole world. His followers became the church. The story of the early Christians is told in *Acts.* The *letters* written to New Testament churches, and the book of *Revelation*, show how the Christian life can be lived out in a world which still rejects the message of Jesus. No wonder this book is unique!

John completes his Gospel by telling us the purpose of his writing:

"
Jesus performed many other miracles which are not written down in this book. But these have been written in order that you may believe that Jesus is the Messiah, the Son of God, and that through your faith in him you may have life.
JOHN 20:30–31
"

Cliff Richard

the British pop star, says:

'As far as I am concerned the Bible is God's word to his creation, and for truth about him — and about ourselves — it is one hundred per cent reliable . . . With my erratic schedule, it's difficult to set aside a regular time each day for Bible reading. Usually I try to do some study before going to bed . . . The important thing is to come to the Bible expecting to discover something relevant, vital and lasting.'

Charles Schulz

the cartoonist and creator of Charlie Brown and Snoopy, remembers studying the Bible with a group of people at his local church. He says:

'. . . I cannot point to a specific time of dedication to Christ, I was just suddenly "there" . . . I cannot fail to be thrilled every time I read the things that Jesus said, and I am more and more convinced of the necessity of following him.'

Appollo Maweja

was serving a life sentence for murder in a Zaire gaol, chained to another man who was a Christian.

'At night he would tell me of his Saviour . . . I acquired a Bible but it was discovered and burned. Two other prisoners . . . helped me daily by carrying their portion of the scriptures under their prison pullovers. I surrendered to Jesus . . . now I can do nothing but serve him and praise him whose willing prisoner I am forever.'

Manny Brotman

was an orthodox Jew:

'I read in the scriptures that God would send a perfect sacrifice to atone for my sins, one called the Messiah. But how could I know who this Messiah would be? Then, in the Jewish Bible, I saw all the prophecies which identified him . . . I knew that only one person in all history could seriously be considered — Yeshua, known to the Gentiles as Jesus.'

Roger 'Bomba'

was a top radio broadcaster in the Philippines. Bomba was arrested and put in prison for his Marxist views. Looking for something to read in the prison library, he took out a red-covered book.

He was disappointed to find that it was a Bible but he began to read it and found he could not stop. It was not long before he became a Christian and began preaching in the gaol.

After ten years, during which thousands of men came to faith in Jesus, he was released.

READING YOUR OWN BIBLE

> **Your word is a lamp to guide me and a light for my path.**
> PSALM 119:105

The first thing is to get a Bible. You may have been given one by some well-meaning relative — and all you have to do is to blow off the dust! But make sure it is in a version you can understand. There are now so many new ones on the market that it would be a pity to be put off by old-fashioned words. If you do not know which to choose, try the Good News Bible.

You may be the sort of person who can't get on with reading. A comic-strip version might be better — at least to get you started. Or there are books of Bible stories with lots of illustrations, or cassettes and records.

WHERE TO START

There must be many people who have started out full of enthusiasm — begun at Genesis 1, started to flag by Exodus, and been lost without trace somewhere in Leviticus, if they make it that far! Use the contents list at the beginning of your Bible and the 'What is the Bible?' chart to help you find your way around, and decide what you would like to read about first.

If you have never read the Bible before and want to find out about Jesus, start with the shortest Gospel — Mark. Or read Luke's Gospel and then his exciting story of the first Christians in Acts.

To get the taste of the Old Testament, you will find some of the most famous Bible stories in Genesis. Then you might read the stories of Moses (in Exodus) and David (in 1 and 2 Samuel). Try some of the Psalms, too, for prayers and songs of praise.

You will then find the New Testament letters come to life. Try Paul's closely argued letter to the Romans, or one of the more personal letters, such as Philippians.

WAYS TO READ

Everyone is different and there are no rules about how the Bible should be read. You may like to take it in chunks, to get the over-all idea of a passage or a little at a time each day. You might prefer to study and discuss it with other people in a church group or Sunday school, or with your family or a brother, sister or friend.

Here is one way to read it on your own.

● Before you start, pray that God will speak to you.
● Read a short section carefully.
● Think about what it means.
● Decide how to act on what you have learned.

QUESTIONS TO ASK YOURSELF

● What kind of book is the one I'm reading? (Remember, the Bible is a library.)
● Why was it written?
● What did it say to the original readers?
● What does it say to me?

> Now you've told me all about it, I'm really interested. What shall I do next?

> Read it!

WHERE TO TURN

FAMOUS PARTS OF THE BIBLE

Creation of the world   *Genesis 1–3*
Ten Commandments   *Exodus 20:1–17*
'The Lord is my shepherd . . .'   *Psalm 23*
Isaiah's vision of God   *Isaiah 6*
Jesus' death foretold   *Isaiah 53*
The birth of Jesus   *Matthew 1–2; Luke 2*
The Sermon on the Mount   *Matthew 5–7*
The Lord's Prayer   *Luke 11:2–4*
The Last Supper   *Matthew 26:17–30;*
    1 Corinthians 11:23–25
Jesus' death   *Mark 15; Matthew 27;*
    Luke 23; John 19
His resurrection   *Matthew 28;*
    Mark 16; John 20–21; Luke 24
His ascension   *Acts 1:1–11*
The coming of the Holy Spirit   *Acts 2*
Love, the greatest thing in the world
    1 Corinthians 13
John's vision of Jesus   *Revelation 1:9–20*

WHEN YOU NEED HELP

How to pray   *Luke 11:1–13*
Words to praise God   *Psalms 96–100*
What is God really like?
    Isaiah 40:12–31; John 14:8–31
Who was Jesus?   *Matthew 16:13–20*
Why did he come to earth?   *John 3:16–21*
How to become a Christian   *Romans 10:9–13*
What happens when we die?   *John 11:17–27;*
    1 Corinthians 15:35–44; 2 Corinthians 5
When you are lonely or unhappy   *Psalm 23;*
    Luke 24:13–35; Matthew 28:20
When you are worried   *Matthew 6:24–34*
A quick prayer, when in trouble
    Psalm 57 or 70
A prayer for forgiveness   *Psalm 51*
    (also about forgiveness   *1 John 1:8–2:2*)
When you need guidance   *Psalm 25:4–10*
About peace   *John 14:27–29;*
    Philippians 4:6–7

Index